Mom, Mama, and Me...
and How I Came to Be!

Written by Tina Rella
Illustrated by Monica Meza

Produced by Molly Summer
and Guess Who? Multimedia

Guess Who? Multimedia

www.GuessWhoMultimedia.com

Mom is chef, and makes me food I love to eat.

Mama is a writer, and her stories sure are neat!

Mom and Mama love me so, and tell me every day.
I'm the apple of their eyes in every single way!

I love my Mama and Mom –
they make it twice the fun.
Twice the laughs. Second to none...
And I'm glad I'm their son.

Mama reads me stories every night before bed,
She tells me that she loves me as she kisses my head.

Whenever I get scared, Mama's always there.
Mom and Mama always show me that they care.

If I'm feeling sad, Mom can make me giggle.
By tickling my toes and making me wiggle!

With Mama and Mom, it's twice the hugs,
and I'm twice as happy.
With my Mama and Mom, I feel so snappy!

'Cause two is better than one...
Having two moms is way more fun!
I have two moms and I'm twice as glad-

Jonathan didn't know what to say.

Later that night, Jonathan, Mom, and Mama
sat down to eat some of Mom's yummy lasagna.

"Do I have a Daddy?" he asked
as he sat wide-eyed and curious.

"Why do you ask that, honey?" smiled Mama. "Today at school everyone was talking about their dads. "

"I see..." replied Mom. "You know, a family is like a recipe in some ways. Each member is an important ingredient and together, they make something wonderful for everyone to enjoy. But not all recipes are the same."

When someone asks "Where's your dad?"
You'll tell them this, and be so glad -
Your two mamas love you so,
From your head down to your little toe.

Love makes a family, yes it's true.
Love makes a family – me and you.
There's nothing better we could have done-
We always knew that you were the one!

Our prayers and wishes all came true,
When nine months later – there was you!

So when you're asked, once in a while,
Tell them with a smile that your
Two mamas love you so –
And would never ever let you go.
Love makes a family you'll say –
And that's what matters anyway!

Made in the USA
Lexington, KY
14 February 2013